HALLOWEEN

Written by Alice K. Flanagan

Illustrated by Patrick Girouard

Content Adviser: Professor Sherry L. Field, Department of Social Science Education, College of Education, The University of Georgia

Reading Adviser: Dr. Linda D. Labbo, Department of Reading Education, College of Education, The University of Georgia

COMPASS POINT BOOKS

MINNEAPOLIS, MINNESOTA

Compass Point Books
3722 West 50th Street, #115
Minneapolis, MN 55410

Visit Compass Point Books on the Internet at *www.compasspointbooks.com*
or e-mail your request to *custserv@compasspointbooks.com*

Editors: E. Russell Primm and Emily J. Dolbear
Designer: The Design Lab

Library of Congress Cataloging-in-Publication Data

Flanagan, Alice K.
   Halloween / written by Alice K. Flanagan ; illustrated by Patrick Girouard.
   p. cm. — (Holidays and festivals)
  Includes bibliographical references and index.
  ISBN 0-7565-0086-9 (hardcover : lib. bdg.)
   1. Halloween—Juvenile literature. [1. Halloween. 2. Holidays.] I. Girouard,
Patrick, ill. II. Title. III. Series.
  GT4965F53 2002
  394.2646—dc21   2001001505

Table of Contents

"Trick-or-Treat!" Boo! You scare me on Halloween, and I'll scare you.

Halloween is celebrated every year on October 31. On that day, many people decorate their houses with pumpkins and imaginary ghosts. Some adults and children wear costumes and masks. They go door-to-door to get candy. They have fun. But long ago, Halloween was not fun at all.

4

When Did Halloween Begin?

Halloween began more than 2,000 years ago. People called Celts lived in what is now England, Ireland, Scotland, Wales, and northern France.

The Celts **worshiped** many gods. One god was named Samhain. The Celts believed that Samhain called dead people to walk the earth on October 31. The Celts held a **festival** for Samhain on that day. They made October 31 the last day of the Celtic year.

In the evening, the Celts built fires to warm the good spirits. They put out food and other gifts to welcome them. Each family thought about loved ones who had died.

No one welcomed the bad spirits though. They feared them. They believed that bad spirits came to pick who would die during the year. So on the night of October 31, most people wore masks to hide from the bad spirits. They also wore masks to scare the spirits away.

A Feast to Honor the Sun

The festival of Samhain took place on the last day of the Celtic year. The next day was November 1—the first day of the new Celtic year.

On this day, the Celts held a festival for Baal. Baal was god of the sun. The Celts believed that Baal gave the world warmth and light. Without the sun, animals and crops would die, and people would starve. So the Celts thanked Baal.

In November, people could see the sun setting earlier each day. They felt the weather getting colder. They thought the sun was losing its strength and dying.

So on November 1, the Celts built huge fires called bonfires. They gave food to the sun. They believed that food and the fire made the sun strong. The sun needed strength to live through the winter. In the spring, the sun would return with warmth and light.

The Roman Festival

The Romans lived near the Celts, in Italy. They also held a festival on November 1. Their festival honored a **goddess** named Pomona.

The Romans believed that Pomona watched over their crops. They pictured her as a beautiful young woman carrying fruit. She wore a crown of apples on her head. The Romans danced and played games at their festival. They thanked Pomona for being good to them. They passed around apples and nuts in her honor.

The Romans fought the Celts in France. They ruled the Celts for 400 years. During this time, the Romans and the Celts celebrated the festivals of Samhain and Pomona together.

How Did Halloween Get Its Name?

By the ninth century, a new religion had spread around the world. It was called Christianity. People who believe that Jesus Christ is the son of God are called Christians.

Soon, Christians were celebrating the Roman-Celtic festival on November 1, too. But they celebrated it in a new way. On this day, they honored the lives of the saints. Saints were holy men and women. They helped many people. The Christians called their festival All Saints' Day, or All Hallows' Day.

The night before All Hallows' Day was October 31. Christians called this night All Hallows' Even. Later, that name was shortened to Halloween. November 2—the day after All Hallows' Day—was called All Souls' Day. On this day, Christians prayed for souls who were not saints.

The Day of the Dead

In Mexico, people honor the souls of the dead in a special way. On the night of November 1, women and young girls bring food to the cemeteries. They light candles. Then they offer food to the souls of their **relatives**. The men and boys stand outside the cemetery gates and sing.

In the morning, the men and women meet at the graves. Everyone eats the food they have brought. They pray for the spirits of their relatives.

Halloween in North America

About 500 years ago, many people from Europe came to North America. They brought Halloween **customs** with them.

Today, some Christians take part in All Saints' Day and All Souls' Day. But most people just have fun on Halloween. They wear masks and costumes. Some have parties. Others go trick-or-treating door-to-door. Many families decorate their homes with pumpkins, ghosts, and witches. These are the symbols of Halloween.

Some parents go trick-or-treating with their children to make sure they are safe. Other people take their children trick-or-treating in stores or shopping malls. Some children are not allowed to go trick-or-treating door-to-door. Instead, they go to Halloween parties at school or at a friend's house.

Trick-or-Treating

The custom of trick-or-treating may have started in England or Ireland. Long ago in Ireland, religious leaders dressed in costumes. Then they knocked on people's doors. They asked for food or money to give to a powerful spirit named Muck Olla. They said harm would come to anyone who refused. Most people were afraid, so they gave food or money.

Years later, many people became Christians. Then this custom changed.

On All Hallows' Even, some Christians dressed up as saints. Other Christians dressed up as devils. They put on colorful plays called **pageants**. Over time, the custom of wearing costumes was combined with the custom of treat-or-treating.

In England on Halloween night, children dressed up in costumes. They begged for cakes for the dead and treats for the goblins. If the people in the house didn't give them a treat, the children played a trick on them. Sometimes they unlocked the fence gates. Sometimes they let animals out of the barn.

In France, children begged for flowers. Then they used the flowers to decorate churches or the graves of loved ones.

Things You Might See on Halloween Day

Witches on Broomsticks

What do you think of when you think of Halloween? Do you picture a witch on a broomstick and a black cat by her side? The word *witch* comes from an old Saxon word meaning "wise one."

Long ago, women in Europe always carried a pole or a broom when they went for a walk in the country. They used these poles and brooms to help them jump across brooks and streams.

In those days, people believed witches could fly. They thought witches used their brooms to lift them off the ground. When they were in the air, they would fly away on their brooms.

People used to believe that witches got together twice a year. They met on April 30 and on the night of October 31. People said witches danced around bonfires. Before morning, they hopped on their brooms and flew home.

Many people believed that witches got their powers from the devil. They mixed magic brews, or **potions**, in giant pots called **cauldrons**.

Black Cats

No one knows for sure why black cats are often pictured with witches. Maybe it's because witches were said to come out at night with their cats. In the dark, everything looks black, so over time, everyone thought witches' cats were always black. Many others believed that witches could change themselves into cats!

Bats

Over time, bats have become part of the Halloween story, too. It started with the festival of Samhain. People saw bats flying over their bonfires. The bats were hunting insects that were attracted by the flames. Later, people said that bats came out only on Halloween.

Ghosts and Goblins

Many of our ideas about ghosts and goblins came from the festival of Samhain and All Saints' Day. On those days, people believed that evil spirits walked the earth in many forms.

The Irish called the evil spirits banshees and leprechauns. Sometimes they called them fairies and little people. The French called the evil spirits goblins. But they may not have been evil spirits at all.

According to legend, dwarfs lived in the forests of northern Europe. Dwarfs are very small people. These dwarfs lived in small huts with grass roofs. They wore green clothing—the color of the forest—so they would not be seen.

People were afraid of the dwarfs because they were different. Sometimes, travelers thought they saw a dwarf, then—poof!—the dwarf disappeared.

People called it magic. Before long, many people thought dwarfs were evil. They called the dwarfs names, and they made up stories about them.

Pumpkins

Long ago in Ireland, people believed evil spirits were afraid of light. So, to keep away the evil spirits on Halloween, people made lanterns. They cut the center out of turnips and put candles in them.

After the Irish came to America, pumpkins were easier to find. So they used pumpkins instead of turnips. They called the lighted pumpkins jack-o'-lanterns.

Today, people carve faces in pumpkins. The faces can look funny or scary.

What You Can Do
on Halloween Day

Long ago, people honored the souls of the dead on October 31. They put out food to welcome the good souls. They wore ugly masks to scare away the bad ones. The next day, they celebrated the beginning of a new year with dancing and feasting. Today, our celebration of Halloween is a mixture of these customs.

It's fun to wear a costume. It's great going door-to-door to get candy, too. Most of us enjoy ourselves on Halloween.

There are other ways to mark the day. We can do things for others. Here are some ideas:

* Offer to take your little brother or sister trick-or-treating.
* Remember to thank people who give you candy.

* Ask an adult to help you carve a pumpkin. Give it to a friend.
* Help your teacher decorate the classroom for Halloween.
* Put flowers on a relative's grave.
* Ask your parents or teachers to help you collect money for "Trick-or-Treat for UNICEF." To find out more, write to:

The U.S. Fund for UNICEF

Dept. 3064P

P.O. Box 98006

Washington, DC 20090-8006

Or go to their Web site at *http://www.unicefusa.org/trickortreat/* UNICEF stands for the United Nations International Children's Emergency Fund. The group gives needy children food, clean water, medicine, and education. Your efforts on Halloween can help young people around the world.

Glossary

cauldrons large cooking pots used by witches

customs things that members of a group usually do

festival a holiday or celebration

goddess a female god

pageants plays or performances

potions magic mixtures

relatives family members

worshiped loved as a god

Where You Can Learn More About Halloween

At the Library

Barth, Edna. *Witches, Pumpkins, and Grinning Ghosts.* New York: The Seabury Press, 1972.

Berg, Elizabeth. *Festivals of the World: USA.* Milwaukee, Wis.: Gareth Stevens Publishing, 1999.

Chambers, Catherine. *All Saints, All Souls, and Halloween.* Austin, Tex.: Raintree Steck-Vaughn, 1997.

Hintz, Martin, and Kate Hintz. *Halloween: Why We Celebrate It the Way We Do.* Mankato, Minn.:
Capstone Press, 1996.

On the Web

HALLOWEEN ON THE NET: *http://www.holidays.net/halloween/*

For information about Halloween crafts and recipes

HAUNTED HOMEPAGE: *http://www.hauntedhome.com/theHouse/index.htm*

For Halloween safety tips, spooky sounds, and a haunted house

Index

About the Author and Illustrator

Alice K. Flanagan writes books for children and teachers. Since she was a young girl, she has enjoyed writing. She has written more than seventy books. Some of her books include biographies of U.S. presidents and their wives, biographies of people working in our neighborhoods, phonics books for beginning readers, and informational books about birds and Native Americans. Alice K. Flanagan lives in Chicago, Illinois.

Patrick Girouard has been drawing and painting for many years. He lives in Indiana.